Close To My Heart

poems by
Dorthy Knouse Koepke

To my dear Luther clan,
— My mother's book.
Judy Koepke
Spring 2012

ACKNOWLEDGEMENTS

I am grateful to the publications where some of these poems first appeared:

Christian Science Monitor, Whole Notes, Midwest Poetry Review, National Writer's Club, This Day Magazine, Grit Magazine, Nebraska Center for the Book, Lutheran Witness, Celebrate - University of Nebraska-Omaha, and *South Dakota State Poetry Society - Pasque Petals.*

Copyright 2010 by Dorthy Knouse Koepke, Norfolk, Nebraska
All rights reserved.

Book design and layout by Lana Koepke Johnson,
Koepke Design, Lincoln, Nebraska.

LIBRARY OF CONGRESS CATALOGING-IN-PUBLICATION DATA
Koepke, Dorthy Knouse.
Close To My Heart: by Dorthy Knouse Koepke
ISBN: 978-0-557-55153-8

FIRST EDITION

Published by Lulu Enterprises, Inc.
http://www.lulu.com/

for my late husband Herman,
who gave a lifetime of encouragement and adoration for my writing

for my children,
Judy, Janis, JoAnn, Galen, Gary, Gene, Lonnie, Lana, Lynne and Jeffrey,
their spouses,
and my many, amazingly talented, grandchildren,
who provided me with endless material and inspiration

for all my dear friends and relatives,
who also gave me inspiration and encouragement
to record my life and improve my writing

for my grandson Jesse,
who did a superb job of editing this book

for my daughter Lana,
who worked with me to make this book possible

Dorthy Knouse Koepke's well-titled collection of poems, *Close To My Heart*, is a loving memoir of farm life and family. "Farms are poems waiting to be written," she writes in "Poetic Treasure," and from the first poem in the collection, "The Heart Remembers," Koepke's images begin "stamping a farm's soul on memory's heart." I'm sure that anyone with a connection to rural life in the not-so-distant past will find these poems recalling familiar experiences, just as the warm images that culminate in "the busy peacefulness" of "A Barn At Night" recall for me the wealth of sensory experience that emanated from my uncle's barn in the Sandhills each summer evening at milking time.

A love song to life through the course of its ups and downs, *Close To My Heart* reflects a full range of emotional experience. There are poems celebrating warmth, joy and family, alongside those dealing with loneliness, loss and regret. The sudden fear when a circus tent comes down just as the big cats are being released, or when a farm family hears on the radio that a tornado has been reported on the ground nearby, is relieved when the family at the circus is safe again in their car, and when the family on the farm is together down in their storm cellar, out of harm's way. There are reflections on tragic losses – of family members, friends, the little country school – and the sudden awakening of a mother when a near-tragedy is averted.

Koepke's "Elegy For Memorial Day," near the end of this collection, should be required reading for every American, and especially for those now involved in or intending to become involved in politics. If it were memorialized by every American president, and recited in Arlington National Cemetery each year on Memorial Day, it might yet awaken this sleeping giant of a country to a sense of faith, wisdom and love that seems missing now in much of America, but that is still very much alive in many people's memories, and certainly right at home in this collection, *Close To My Heart*.

From poems such as "The Lost Songs," "Cabin Fever" and "Regret" to those titled "What My Grandmothers Taught Me,"

"Meditations Of An Old Woman," and "Serenity," there is a stoic sense of faith, an ever-growing sense of wisdom, and an overwhelming sense of love regarding the course of life. After asking in one poem, "Why did I marry and live on the farm…?" the poet ends each stanza with her answer, which is also the title of the poem, "Love Made Me Do It," It is obvious that this entire collection of poems had the same genesis.

Thank you, Dorthy, for the memories.

Neil Harrison
English Instructor
Humanities, Arts & Social Sciences
Northeast Community College
Norfolk, Nebraska

Contents

Farm

The Heart Remembers 2

The Rain Wind 4

Love Song To My Tired Retired Husband 5

Revival 6

A Barn At Night 7

Busy Morning At The Farm And Ranch
Supply Building Supply 8

Love Made Me Do It 9

Dustbowl 10

Cycle Of Seasons 12

Prairie Blizzard 13

Soul Journey 14

Observations On Farmers 15

Song Of The Farm 16

Mud Prints 18

A Farmer Has No Use For Poets 19

The Lost Songs 20

Poetic Treasure 22

Ice Storm 25

Brush Pile 26

Return Of Spring 27

Apple Orchard Delirium 28

Plea Bargain 29

April's Apples 30

Storm Cellar 31

My Speckled Hen 33

Beauty 34

Family

Sign Language 36

Grandpa's Boy 37

How Do I Tell My Son? 38

The Night The Tent Blew Down 39

Sixteen 40

The Carousel 41

The Little White School 42

The Journey 43

Mountain Stream 45

Fisherman's Delight 46

Going Home 47

Serenity 48

My Peony 49

Day Alone 50

The Awakening 51

The Bicycle Rider 52

Autobiography Of A Writer 53

Resurrection	54
The Leveling	55
Regret	58
What My Grandmother Taught Me	59
A Day With Rebecca	61
Loaves Of Love	64
A Dress For Granddaughter's Wedding	66
Shuttling Grandma	67
Renewal	68
Nightmares	69
Cabin Fever	70
The Accommodating Accomplice	71
J. Willy Wunder And Model T	73
Oracle On Oracles	75
Unrequited Love	76
Strawberry Pie	77
The Catalyst	78
Elegy For Memorial Day	79
Mediations Of An Old Mother	81
Pain	82
Devotion	83
Let It Be Spring	84
Farewell To Dear Friend	85
About The Author	89

Close To My Heart

I. Farm

The Heart Remembers

Something special about stamping
a farm's soul on memory's heart;
long ago time of lamp light,
and days of familiar routines;
of waking with the dawn,
listening to vocal greetings of animals,
and busy conversation of birds;
cool breezes whispering benedictions
through cottonwood leaves,
litanies of praise for God's benevolence,
gift of hope for a bright new day.

Memories of squeezing streams
of milk from cud-chewing cows,
frothing foam in sturdy buckets,
an audience of hungry cats waiting
for a sure breakfast; of cranking
the cream separator handle, faster
and faster, until the ding-ding bell
hushed, and cream, thick and rich,
and anemic skim milk flowed down
private spouts into separate pails.

Of feeding milk to bucket calves,
slobbering on fingers, mistaken for
nipples; of slopping sows, squealing
and pushing at hog pen troughs;
of opening the hen house door,
releasing a daily panorama of
white sails flying across the yard.

Finally, breakfast of hot cakes, bacon, eggs,
purple prunes, half submerged in thick
cream, like out-of-place humpback whales,
steaming cups of coffee, fresh ground,

stewed in gray pots on the corn-cob fired
kitchen range that landscaped the oil-clothed
table; fueled for our muscle-and-sweat day.

Then taking precedence over breakfast
dishes stacked on the kitchen table,
lamps, relieved of night's sentry duty,
gathered from stations throughout
the house, were refilled with
kerosene; globes, smoked up by oily
breath of flickering wicks, were made
ready for nightfall; washed in soapy
hot water, polished with flour sack
towels until they sparkled in the sun.

When shadows began to creep in
through twilight darkened windows,
the kitchen lamp, clusters of lavender
lilacs playing ring-around-the-rosy
on its porcelain base, enthroned as
table centerpiece; wafted faint scents
of burning wick; its thrifty beam of
light, afraid to venture into dark
corners, proved ever faithful to
illuminate our evening rituals.

Our time to write, lessons, letters,
our time to feast on wonders of books,
newspaper, treasured magazines,
the Bible's wisdom, content in our
closed circle of togetherness.

The Rain Wind

Listen to the moaning, the wild
eerie moaning of the rain wind,
sounding the slats on the patio trellis
like strings on a sobbing violin.

Where did the rain wind learn its song,
its melancholy moaning under my eaves,
around house corners and deep window wells,
its wailing through the pin oak's leaves?

How does the rain wind know when to sing
in tune with the mourning dove's call,
when bright sun blazes in thistle-down skies,
how does the wind know rain will soon fall?

Love Song To My Tired Retired Husband

You ride the sun of the morning,
Escaping this home newly urban,
Returning to the place of your childhood,
Denying its era must end,
The roots of your going entangled,
The now intertwined with the then.

This is your life you are saying,
Sweat dripping sweet on your brow,
The plow running straight in the furrow,
The smell of soil in your soul,
Earth's greening your reason for living.

My love, your old joints thicken,
Like a horse that has plodded too long,
Your nights are tortured by cramping,
Exhaustion your constant companion,
Ears deaf to the birds' bright song.

It is your heart for which I am longing,
I wait for its glad coming home,
For this, your now fickle lover,
In the end will nurture your failing
And taunt infirmities' toll.

Stay with me in the dawn of your mornings,
Let my love be the rain for your greening,
Let my heart be your fresh-turned sod,
Let me kiss the sweet flesh of your sparse-rooted head,
And I will wash it with tears of thanksgiving.

Then we shall rejoice in the bounty
Of the harvest now ready for gleaning,
Of our faith, our reason for being,
Of our love, our lifeline for living,
Taproot for all future vining,
Legacy for posterity's spring.

Revival

See how straight the flowers stand
In joyous adoration,
When only yesterday they lay
Thirsted to prostration,
Then the Lord stretched out His hand,
Sent gentle rain across the land
Most of the night,
Now see how straight the flowers stand
In morning light.

A Barn At Night

There is something peaceful about a barn at night,
something musical in all the ordinary sounds
as animals in random weariness settle down.

With rhythmic chewing of cuds,
drowsing cattle drop ponderous bodies
on bedding straw crackling,
their busy innards rumbling
in harmony with saddle ponies munching
last morsels of grain from feed box corners,
while prowling cats rustle across the hay,
eyes radar-beamed for careless mice.

Slumbering pigeons rouse on lofty perches
and coo contentedly in the cupula,
as moon ribbons glisten through frosted windows
stirring faint shafts of light into soft shadows,
gathering in all the busy peacefulness
of a barn at night.

Busy Morning At The Farm & Ranch Building Supply

The pay loader aims corrugated steel
at the rear of my Volare and misses
my wheel by an inch. The carpenters
load wooden feed bunks on flatbed trucks,
restrain them in a strait jacket cinch,

and hang red flags on the end like pot hole
warnings or beware of mean dog signs. Like
cooks breaking long spaghetti into a pot,
saws whine in the steel shed slicing 4 by 4's
into precise lengths for toe-tapping customers.

Men in red sweatshirts run up and down steps,
in and out of the office, like gerbils
in a cage fitted with exercise wheels,
and put bolts in trunks of Chevies and planks
and wire netting in Ford pickup boxes.

My husband vanished into the office
an hour ago to ask the price of steel siding.
The sun grows hot enough for mischief and
microwaves my arm through the car window
while I wait, a prisoner in this man's world,

envious of the surprise train whistling
tornado sirens as it earthquakes by
on the track beside me, much too shrewd
to get involved with a busy morning
at the Farm & Ranch Building Supply.

Love Made Me Do It

Why did I marry and live on the farm,
Awakened at dawn by a clanging alarm?
Why did I milk in a cold drafty stall,
When farming was not my lifestyle at all?
Before we were married, really, I knew it,
Then why did I wed? Love made me do it!

My darling, who promised I'd be his queen,
Sent me to wash with his mother's machine,
He upped his production down on the farm,
Including ten babies crooked in my arm,
Work and more work, he kept adding to it,
Why did I stay? Love made me do it!

With diapers and doughnuts, chickens and cows,
Cooking and weeding, and slopping the sows,
Gardens and haying, and lunches for men,
Over, and over, and over again,
All the while knowing that I really blew it,
Why did I stay? Love made me do it!

Dustbowl

Poverty walks barefoot
in the snow, and wraps
in cast-off clothes
when winter's winds blow cold,
and hunger's sunken ribs
consume thin milk, bled
from feeble cows, nosing thistles
pushed down from dusty haymows.

Gray sheets drip on windows
thrust against the parched noon,
trapping wild dust,
dust forever blowing,
creating desert dunes,
burying fences, burying bones
growing where wheat dispenses
with harvest.

Desolation grows blind eyes
to save senses from madness,
hope lies without meaning,
shrouded in grave clothes,
and the sun's white heat
sires phantom horses, who sweep
across the horizon, spawning
dust devils, flouting
the prairie's barrenness.

Prosper the green land,
God of plenty, overflow
the outstretched hand, that my loves
might never know, how cold
the night wind blows,

while the day burns, and no one
knows where the seasons go,
when hunger rides the cold, cold wind,
and poverty walks barefoot
in the snow.

Cycle Of Seasons

Scattered clouds hasten across winter's gray sky,
helpless to resist the force of the north wind,
and I am thankful for the whistling of hot air
through the furnace ducts. Nothing better right now
than to be sitting at my kitchen table,
digging my fork into a mound of vegetables,
stacked like a miniature pile of colored corn
at a country elevator.

The deep gold of carrots, the blonde gold of corn,
Emerald peas, and rich green of French cut beans,
and pale green baby limas. I close my eyes
and remember the feel of soft earth sifting
through my fingers, the spring planting of seed,
in long shallow furrows made by string-guided hoes,
and the smell of the bounty at harvest time,
preserved in the forever winter of the freezer.

And finally at journey's end on my plate,
nourishing my body, gift of a loving God.
Winter is the earth's time of resting,
and I will not sing a melancholy song
now that the sky grows dreary, or harmonize
with the wail of the north wind, for, without fail,
this season of winter will pass, and spring will come.

Prairie Blizzard

The blizzard stalks the snow-blinded prairie
like some predator making powerless its prey.
It sweeps with frost teeth across fields
and valleys, and roars through farmsteads
and bare branched cottonwoods.

White-faced Herefords hunch,
rounded rumps defying the wild wind,
fresh-dropped calves huddle under cow bellies,
steamy vapors escape from frosted nostrils,
and dissipate in the storm's breath.

The storm tatters night's curtains
into white shreds, its icicle gales
fling snow brutally, piling high mountains
where none were yesterday.

Rock hard, the snowdrifts, thrust
into intricate patterns, glisten
with sun crystals at day's dawning
wrapped in warming rays of morning sun,
wet hides steam and drip amber rivers,
hungry calves nuzzle their mothers.

Soul Journey

I have need of a day at dawn,
learning the bank of the river
with a bamboo pole in my hands,
a sinker to anchor the bobbing cork
no hook on the end of the line,
just the sound of water lapping
on shaded shore,
the brush of breeze on my face,
enough cloud to dim the sun,
a grassy seat, a cottonwood tree
to lean on, no fish biting
to disturb my meditation,
to renew my soul again.

Observations On Farmers

A farmer can be so practical.
His thoughts can dwell
on mud and mire,
stench of animals,
and he can forget the musky scent
of fresh mown hay,
and the heavenly peace of dawn
sliding off the lap of night
over quiet hills.
He can remember dust and heat,
itching flesh, and money
lost or gained,
and forget that wind-swept fields
of grain, and rustling green of corn,
are not his creation.

Song Of The Farm

Farms are good places to be,
although farms smell,
and not always of clover.
Most everything on the farm
is fun to play with
and work to clean up after,
and some things are dangerous
to be around, but you can have
ten dogs and twenty cats,
and pigs and cows,
and your neighbors don't mind
as long as you keep your animals
behind fences and care for them.

Every child is exposed
to sex education, because everyone
is exposed to the miracle
of life and death;
something is always being born,
and something is always dying.

Woods camp behind our house,
hills beckon to be run over,
cherries beg to be picked,
ponies abound to jog on,
and dogs are thick to hunt with.
But wind and cold,
and fickle rain,
and hail and snow,
and insects and diseases
keep us mindful of the Lord.

A farm child never says
to his mother "What can I do?"
because he knows,
gardens need to be hoed,

weeds need to be chopped,
cows have to be milked,
pigs have to be fed,
barns have to be cleaned,
and cattle have to be moved
from one pasture to another.
In fact, there are enough jobs
to keep one busy right through
the twenty-first century.

Yes. A farm child learns
young, to never ask
what can I do; he knows
he had better be quiet,
if he wants to do some things
that he likes to do, and not
just what has to be done;
though sometimes he gets paid,
though not much,
for doing fun things
some people travel miles for,
and even pay for,
while others can only pace
on some bleak street
and wait for heaven.

Mud Prints

Just watch that mischievous sun
microwave the snow
to mud puddled
evidence of spring,
ink jets for child-feet
to print tracks
across my kitchen floor.

Almost a dozen printers
have already passed this way.
Now their type fonts
have enlarged, and they remember
not to track mud
across shiny floors
in other places.

I headline their courage
to leave childhood's safe nest
and walk bravely into the unknown,
yet I allow myself a little sadness,
and on spring days
I am also a bit lonely.

But my perception of those remaining
is more acute, and instead of
fretting about mud prints,
I concentrate more on the sunshine,
and the snow going,
and spring coming,
and the laughter of grandchildren
printing tracks of happiness
across my kitchen floor.

A Farmer Has No Use For Poets (Haying – 1950's Style)

A farmer has no use for poets, when hot hangs the day,
And sweat streams muddy furrows down his weary dusty face.
He thinks of no sweet-scented words as he works at stacking hay,
For where the roaring hay sweep races, a poet has no place.

Yet the farmer sniffs the sun-cured hay, and his tired body thrills
As the horses strain to lift the loaded stacker gliding high,
And the hay bunch falls by the farmer crouching careful when it spills,
And quick he jumps to fork it neat in place, and weeps dust from his eye.

When dusk is creeping up close by the stack's dark silhouette,
The farmer, on his homeward way, looks back, and stops to lift his hat,
And proud, he wipes his dirty face, and forgets the hot day's sweat,
Then turns again to sing a song – perhaps a poet is some use at that.

The Lost Songs

Where did the songs go?
The songs of the farmer
tired and worn, riding home
on his load of corn,
singing in the moonlight
on crisp November nights,
keeping time to the clop-clop
of Belgian hooves,
and the wagon wheels'
steady clacking.

Where did the songs go?
The melodies now lacking,
the melodies the farmer's wife
sang as she shared his busy life,
and heard him coming home at night
singing his songs in bright moonlight.

Now the countryside thunders
with giant mechanical wonders
of pickers and combines
that flatten the fields,
Filling their maws
with miraculous yields,
garnering the golden harvest.
At night there is no rest,

amplified radios boom and bump
above the roar of motors,
that growl and thump
vibrating the ground,
shattering eardrums for miles around,
drowning the farmer's joy songs,
destroying his peace and quiet,
until he no longer sings
in the bright moonlight
on crisp November nights.

And what of the farmer's wife,
she no longer hears his song,
she no longer hums her melodies,
she has her stereo on, and waits
for his call on the cellular phone
to let her know he is coming home.

Her serenade the motor's roar,
and his radio thumping
some strange song,
only that and nothing more,
for the farmer coming home
no longer sings his joy songs
in the bright moonlight
on crisp November nights.

Poetic Treasure

Farms are poems
waiting to be written.

Cottonwood leaves dance
to the wind's symphony,
robins and wrens warble and flit,
riding hackberry branches
like trapeze artists.

Summer breezes encourage gyrations
in the meadow's ballerina grass,
cows graze placidly, baby calves appliqué
black and white clumps on green velvet.

Roosters crow at dawn, buglers
of sunrise, hens cackle all morning,
advertising fast food in nests of straw.

Round alfalfa bales dot clipped fields,
share their aroma, like sun-browned loaves
of bread, set out to cool.

Corn leaves rustle and tassels wave,
thick stalks crack with growing pains,
the oat field turns to gold.

Adventurous children brave dark forests
of wind breaks, alert English Shepherds
and protective collies guard their flanks.

Tractors snort and snarl, rumble past patios,
wagging dust clouds behind them,
sweat tunneling murky rivers on faces
mottled with grease and mud, drivers
seek shelter from noontime sun.

Cool splashes of water and soap
and thirsty towels transform weary drivers,
refreshed as dusty earth after rain.

Hunger-driven, they claim their places
around tables groaning with abundance
gathered from freezers, gardens and pantries,
and row on row of rainbow jars,
surprise poems from the heart.

Ice Storm

High line wires glisten with ice,
snap like weak threads under crystal
burdens, and sever the umbilical
cord attached to the power plant.
Their lifeline cut, motors stop,
quieted the monotony of TV,
no blaring of CD's, no washer,
no vacuum, no hot soup.

A subtle peace steals in,
reward of these hours
when time stands still;
until electricity throbs
through the wires again;
grateful for its untimely pausing,
wrapped in down comforters,
I find my meditations vexed
by nagging needles of guilt.

In the frigid white world
outside my glazed windows, my mind
pictures linemen working on high poles,
gloves frosted with ice crystals;
farmers chopping ice from feed bunks,
edging tractors and wagons along side,
scooping steaming silage
to hungry cattle crowding close.

I envision dairy cows, accustomed
to the soft vacuum of milking machines,
startled by cold hands of weary milkers;
trucks roar down streets spewing salt;
snow plows shoot streams of white missiles,
cars slip and slide through slippery streets.
The world goes on, so many brave the cold
to bring convenience back to me.

But then, what do I need of guilt?
Did I not, when I was younger,
suffer the wind's icy chill,
and endure winter's cruel catastrophes?
At fourscore plus five years,
I deserve this warm nest of down,
this gift of peace and relaxation;
posterity carries the torch
and will keep the flame burning.

Brush Pile

A blemish boldly visible,
a brush pile bunches beside the lane;
winds torment its shamble
of twisted branches, dead, brittle,
embedding the twig claws
with tumble weeds.
Sheltered in the heart of it
a red vixen nuzzles her whelps,
transforming the brush pile
into a haven of life and love.

Return Of Spring

We were suspicious at first
when spring came early;
deceived by velvet breeze,
and warmth of sun,
we began to believe
that winter had truly departed
and ceded his reign to her.

Then came a feast of golden daffodils,
tulips, lush with buds,
stood eager to flaunt their
glorious displays, maple leaf buds
threw off rust-red hoods, and wild
plum trees donned lacy shawls.

Abundant rains flushed out
near-drowning earthworms,
fat bodies squiggling patterns
on drive ways and side walks,
scrawling across paved streets;
delight of fishermen and hungry robins.

Gullible as scam victims, basking
in illusions of a permanent reprieve
from polar bear weather, we were
blind-sided by winter's return, watching
in dismay, as icy winds devastated
the raw earth's brief awakening.

Caretaker of God's ravaged world,
spring willed tulips to lift
wilted leaves, surviving buds
to bloom, urged red rhubarb stalks
to revive, early blossomed trees,
now bare, to don green leaf crowns,
and healing winds, and verdant turf,
to repossess the land.

Apple Orchard Delirium

I love apple blossoms in spring,
green-appled trees in summer,
and apples ripe in autumn,
yellow and red, and mottled with green,
sorted in bins in the apple shed.

I savor the flavor of crisp-crunch bites
of scarlet Jonathans, as I watch
the rubber-belted sorting machine roll
the fresh-picked fruit past waiting
workers, expert dividers of perfection
for bins, and culls for bargain basket and cider.

Possessed by apple delirium I buy,
perfection for eating, and the culls,
windfalls, bird bite samplers and knobbies,
for capturing the best of all seasons
in gleaming jars of apple sauce
and spicy butters in my fruit cellar;
to relish on wintry days, when cold winds
swirl drifting snow through the orchard,
and, bare and brittle, the apple trees rest.

Plea Bargain

Please wait, Jack Frost, cancel your
appointment with September. Late October
will grant you ample time to sentence
autumn's loveliness to death. Do not

distress my delicate impatiens, my
delphiniums and dahlias blooming late,
my climbing roses twining vibrant rainbows
above the trellised gate, and lush tomatoes
pinked on optimistic vines. Wait until

the farmers gather in their soybeans and
maize, matured and ready for the bin.
Spare my pumpkins glowing orange in
autumn's sun. Let them linger long through
golden laze of Indian Summer, before
they feel the chill your icy fingers bring.

Please, Jack Frost, this is my plea,
I believe it only fair, since you have
had your way these many years, to grant
this just reprieve, and spare this rare
and glorious autumn especially for me.

April's Apples

In April, from the basement refrigerator,
I salvage the remainder of October's
Jonathans, wrinkled as ancient grandmothers.
Dumped in the peeling pan,
they bump and float in the water.
My thin-bladed paring knife,
dull-crunches around the shriveled circle
of peel, slices through the wilted body,
lifts out the black-seeded core,
and slowly the stewing pot fills.

Spongy quarters of April's apples,
stewing in pineappled syrup,
quench their long winter of thirst,
grow plump and juicy as they were,
in October, lovely and useful
as revitalized grandmothers.

Storm Cellar

Sizzle-fingered lightening
splinters smoky skies,
thunder locomotives rumble
across the earth, roller coaster clouds
dip and swirl in confused directions.

Air pillows stifle our breath
as we hover by the weather radio,
with the expectation of an audience
waiting for the band's first rousing
blast of a John Phillips Sousa march.

The announcer's voice crackles
through the static, "tornado on ground-
immediately take cover."

Family, neighbors, visiting Grandmother
scramble toward the storm cellar,
scurrying down slippery steps
into the dank underground shelter,
to sit among treasures gathered
by anxious children within the hour.

Barbie dolls, toy John Deere tractors,
plastic horse and three-legged cow,
jug of water, containers of cookies,
oatmeal and chocolate chip.

Duchess and newborn puppies whimper
in the padded laundry basket.
Mama Cat cuddles two shivering
kittens in the doll cradle.

Grandmother clings to her prayer book,
and fusses with the tattered old shawl
wrapped securely around the flowered box
holding her special red hat.

We huddle together on moldy benches,
candle light flickers across our faces
as we wait out the storm, snug as gophers
in a burrow; safe from vicious-tongued
winds snapping at us through the cellar vents.

My Speckled Hen

My speckled hen was singing, singing
underneath the purple lilacs,
when suddenly her beady eyes
flashed with ebony fire
as she snatched a quite unwilling
soft white worm
and wound him down
her silky feathered throat
into the dark sea of her craw.

The quite unwilling soft white worm,
squirming and sighing, said
"I have reclined in a multitude of environments
but I am inclined to think
that this one is the pits."

And what about my speckled hen?
She only hiccupped quite discretely
and went on singing, singing
underneath the purple lilacs.

Beauty

My grandfather gave her to my mother
on her wedding day, this sorrel filly,
prancing, neck arched, and gentle-eyed,
a horseman's dream, my mother chose her name,
Beauty, and my father broke her docile as a lamb.

I cannot remember my first time to ride
spraddle-legged and sparkle-eyed behind
my older brother, but I remember riding solo,
scraped off most days by inconvenient
clotheslines, and tops of hen house doorways,
until I grew more clever than my mount.

Time cannot erase that sublime sensation,
the melding of horse and rider,
flowing as one body, motion on motion,
loping long hours across the prairie.
I taste still the sun and wind in my face
and savor the sweet pungent smell of horse,
and feel my pant legs plaster to my skin,
sweat-molded with dust and stitched with
her sorrel hide's shedding of sun rust hair.

Close To My Heart

II. Family

Sign Language

What purpose
the hand uplifted
at the kitchen windows,
like a railroad flagman
routing others
to strange or familiar places.
Some return,
some to never come
or leave again.

Those who will return
go with joy,
and if the Lord should chart
another path for some,
my heart finds peace
in knowing that for both,
my parting words,
my hand waving
at the kitchen window
signed, "I love you."

Grandpa's Boy

He was his Grandpa's little boy,
His Grandpa was his pride and joy.
He could not understand just why
His own dear Grandpa had to die.
He laid his head on Grandpa's chair,
And wept with grief he could not bear.
Oh, Lord, he knew not what to do,
When Grandpa went to live with you.

Beside his window ledge that night,
He knelt to pray in bright starlight,
And as he wiped his tears away,
In wonderment I heard him say,
"I see my Grandpa in the sky,
He's on that cloud that's going by,
He's happy there I plainly see,
Look how he smiles and waves at me."

"My Grandpa's happy there," he said,
With tear-stained face he climbed in bed,
And when he laid him down to sleep,
He closed his eyes and ceased to weep.
With childhood's pure perceptive eyes,
He saw his Grandpa in the skies,
And in the dreamland of his heart,
The two of them will never part.

How Do I Tell My Son?
(That He Has Hodgkin's)

How do I tell my son
the tiny ray of hope
has flickered and burned out?
My mouth is full of ashes.
How do I tell him, Lord,
what fiendish thing
lays hold on him
and seeks to claim his body?

What reason, Lord?
Why pick on him?
Since when is eighteen years
enough of life to give?
Why give him breath at all?
This hallway stretches
cold and bleak, and private hell
may hide behind the doors,
but I hide in the hallway.

My mortal mind is paralyzed
by humanness, fearing pain
the future surely holds for us.
Where are you, Lord? I cannot bear
this agony alone! Did you desert
this sterile place and me?
Please answer, how do I tell my son?

Forgive me, Lord.
I should have known
that while I paced outside his door,
You were waiting, patiently,
beside his bed
with your answer.

The Night The Tent Blew Down

We clung to our mother's skirt and hid,
For we were a frightened bunch of kids,
the night the circus came to town,
and a storm came up and the tent blew down
and the big top toppled in the wind
just as the lion and tigers came in.

The music stopped and the lights went out,
and everyone heard the ringmaster shout,
"Be calm!!" but they paid him not a bit of heed,
and went scrambling out at reckless speed,
as in the darkness workers groped
to grasp the ends of dangling ropes,
while elephants bellowed and lions roared
and storm winds howled and wild rain poured.

We tromped through mud to find our car,
almost too frightened to walk that far,
and cussing the weather my father swore,
he'd grace a circus tent no more.
Oh, we were a bunch of bawling kids,
in the old Model T that slipped and slid,
the night the circus came to town,
and a storm came up and the tent blew down.

Sixteen

Suddenly body conscious,
fascinated with mirrors,
this emerging butterfly,
eager, yet hesitant
to open her wings and fly,
at night, snuggles
back into her cocoon,
cuddling her faded
and tattered baby blanket.

The Carousel

Nothing brings back the child in me,
or anyone else for that matter,
than the sound of a calliope,
with prancing horses, spotted, spattered,
keeping time on the carousel,
holding us all in its magical spell,
reviving memories of going around,
held safely in a prancing steed,
by a parent's arms, thrilling to the sound,
of music, horses marching full speed,
on pipe legs, around and around,
up and down on the merry-go-round.

The Little White School

The little white school on the hillside
Will not open its door in the fall.
The pencil-scarred seats will stand vacant,
And will idle the blackboarded wall.
The halls will be empty and silent
The dust will collect on the floor,
The cobweb will cradle the spider,
And the lock will shackle the door.

The program at Christmas was cherished,
When the parents and neighbors were there
To listen to pieces and playlets,
And childish achievements to share.
The picnic when school year was ended,
And completed were studies and tests,
This friendly assembly of neighbors
Will vanish along with the rest.

The teacher's close ties with her pupils,
Will linger as the years journey on,
Though clamor at noon on the school yard
Will soon be forgotten and gone.
The little white school on the hillside,
From an era more simple and free,
This symbol of life in the country
Was our Statue of Liberty.

The Journey

From Nebraska plains to the Rocky
mountains, and back on the road toward
home, riding over a thousand miles with
three grandchildren, aged five months to ten,
spawned more smiles of remembrance
than a bagel machine shooting out bagels.

Sixty-five years of adventurous journeys,
from graveled roads, pot-holed as Swiss
cheese, only deeper; cars, mobile convection
ovens, with dust-laden winds swirling in
through open windows; to present day
inconvenient hassles, wrinkled unique
experiences into our receptive minds.

At night, sometimes, we bedded down
on old blankets, spread over lumpy grass,
stared up at the night sky, ablaze with an
uncountable maze of stars; tortured by hums
of mosquitoes, drunken from too much
of our blood; listened to howling and
rustling of unseen night creatures; parents
soothed their children, formed an invincible
fortress of love around them; slabs of bread,
cold minced ham, stale coffee, a farmer's
warm milk, sugar cookies, home baked,
appeased hunger, without complaint.

Yet, traveling was a rare excitement,
driving on narrow mountain roads,
partially paralyzed with tingling fear, awed
speechless by first views of deep valleys,
streams gurgling, tumbling down mountains
over water-polished rocks; music of aspens

whispering; sightings of elk or deer grazing
in the meadows, bull moose or black bear,
wrote indelible marks on vacuous memories.

Pot-holed highways became smooth
as table tops, on which we travel,
in automobiles, air-conditioned,
luxurious as royal coaches,
and lounge in plush motels,
dine on gourmet meals.
Alas, addiction to electronic devices,
eyes and ears glued to tiny televisions
hanging above their heads, hand-
held video games, blind children's eyes
to the wonder, the magnificence
of God's creation, only the baby smiled
and chattered, tried to make them see
enchanting wonders of first experience.

Mountain Stream

Spring water
gurgling its birth cry,
newborn progeny of sun
and melting mountain snow
emerging from dissolving drifts,
cradled by worn stream beds,
feeling its way over pebbles
it winds down the mountain,
cascading over waterfalls,
singing a song of ecstasy.

Nectar for the sun,
siphoned off by irrigation canals
and panting cities, it quenches
summer's thirst, and evaporates
like the strength of an old man,
as it trickles into autumn.
Wrapped in the arms of winter,
the stream cradle waits
for another spring,
another birth.

Fisherman's Delight

I feel the creepy wiggle worm,
rebelling, twist and bend and squirm,
while I, so thoughtlessly
quickly end his destiny.

The baited hook becomes a part
of lapping waves, my drowsy eyes
ever on the bobber, floating
and darting in reflected skies.
I dream, and swat the buzzing flies,
and sip contentment's pure delight,
completely taken by surprise,
when fish are prone to take a bite.

The moment that the bobber dives
beneath the waves, I jerk the pole.
A silver flash like dew at dawn,
whose fins and tail have lost control
of motion, lands upon the shore.
I cast again into the shoal,
twice blest, as God renews my store
of food for body, food for soul.

Going Home

Three score and ten years,
since I knew these flat fields,
incapacitated by thirst.
Now they stretch to the far horizon,
an emerald sea, rippled
by the prairie wind.

Here stood, in my childhood,
the paint-starved house
and barn, amid an assortment
of pathetic buildings,
hungry for prosperity.

Dark clouds riding the sky
birthed hope for coming rain,
brought only blowing dust,
taunting us with some cruel joke,
turning our cattle and horses
to bleached bones, while hunger
gnawed in our bellies.

Now all is gone,
and memories fade,
healed by green fields
as far as eyes can see;
rivers of heaven open,
falling rain resuscitates
the prairie's heart,
hope lives again.

Serenity

At dusk
the street is quiet.
I sit on my front steps,
drinking tranquility,
meditating, about God's blessings,
about humdrum duties of days,
about life's twilight.

Somewhere,
in a secret puddle
over behind the Baptist church,
louder than the hum of traffic
on Benjamin Avenue,
the sound of frogs singing
startles me. I savor
their surprise serenade,
and for a moment
I am young again,
sitting on the cistern lid
in the front yard,
meditating at the end of another
exhausting day on the farm,
the moon's reflection grinning
in my kitchen windows.
I feel again the cool south breeze
brushing the sweat from my face,
sweeping away my weariness,
as it strums the hackberry leaves
like some celestial lyre,
softening the exuberant frog chorus
swelling up from the pasture creek.

I lean back now against the step,
listen to the frogs
singing their songs of continuity,
and, serene in the twilight of life,
I am not afraid of the night.

My Peony

My peony beside the garden gate has yet
to bloom; it hesitates to share its redness
with the sun. Perhaps, distressed, my peony
assumes that I would overlook its loveliness.

It noticed that I failed to see my lilacs flower,
splashing lavenders and pinks in emerald leaves;
it knows I did not savor their aroma or fill
my arms with fragrant blossoms in morning's
early hours, as I had always done in other years.

It knows I cut no fresh bouquets to fill the
special crystal vases, dear to my mother long ago;
she, too, loved lilacs so, growing them in
places I remember still; how sad it is, I did not
even think of her this spring when my life hurried
by too fast, and I did not see my lilacs bloom.

Be still my wearied soul and meditate.
Rejoice! The Lord renews the earth once more,
and even though my peony blooms late, spring
still sings its vibrant songs of praise!

As bright sun, after rain, brushes clouds away,
my happiness will soon return these lovely days,
if I but wait a while, remembering my lilacs
will bloom again another spring; now I must
tell my peony it should not hesitate to smile.

Day Alone

The rain mist feathered lullabies
outside my open window throughout the night.
Now at morning light, the family showers sleep
from weary eyes, munch their toast and honey buns
and hasten out into their waiting worlds,
and I am alone, sleeping cat and dog alone.

The raindrops' steady humming becomes staccato
hammering of sleet, and soon thick lines
of falling snow turns greening grass to white.

Divided into gauzy ribbons by shafts
of daylight sifting through half-opened slats of
mini-blinds, the gray angora claims the wicker
sofa's rosebud spattered cushion, while the cocker spaniel
sprawls contented in his master's rocker;
quiescent balls of silken fur, they make this
quiet solitude their customary habit, their only dialogue strange
sound effects to private dreams.

The furnace fan completes its thermostatic duty,
and wall clocks tick away the lazy hours,
reminding me of kitchens long ago, the smell
of apple logs and kettles singing on the fire.

Rest in bed, the doctor said, no strain,
no stress, so here I leave all untidiness
in peace; no concern is mine, no nagging tasks,
except the luxurious pampered care of me,
a convalescent in my daughter's home.

The Awakening

His brothers, by the wild waters,
saved him from dying,
and brought him to me, wet and cold,
still crying.
Thankfully, I held him close
against my breast,
only with my arms around him
could my heart rest.

I half-saw with careless eyes,
and missed, somehow,
my son's endearing ways
until just now.
His very nearness blinded me,
oh, thank you, Lord, I pray,
You opened up my heedless eyes,
keep them this way.

The Bicycle Rider

Shadows that move,
up and down,
around and around.

Hey, fellow,
what if I didn't see you?
Stunt men lack courage
to work in darkness;
only fools are brave enough.

Don't you know
automobiles crunch bicycles,
and people who ride them?

Autobiography of a Writer

My mama, I said, I am a writer,
How lovely, my child, sing me your songs.
Then she shackled my hands with womanly duties,
And warped my young body with hip-riding babies.
My fingers born fashioned for holding a pen
Grew calloused and burned on hot pots and pans.

My husband, I said, I am a writer,
How lovely, my darling, sing me your songs,
I took in my hands long hours of labor,
Cow teats and hog slop, and weeds ever growing.
My fingers born fashioned for gripping a pen
Guided ten children from birth day to altar.

I know, said my husband, you are a writer,
Now we are old, please sing me your songs,
Take in your hands the tools for your writing,
Write me the songs you said you could sing.
Gray hair and shadows, my passion deserts me,
Though my body still lives, my spirit has died.

The evening flames red across the horizon,
Lost are the years time has consumed.
Now gather together my lost inspirations,
Gather them all for the burial rite.
Let the grave swallow up my songs never written
While the night sky burns with my anger.

Resurrection

Summer died bleeding
from slashed veins
of dark-skinned chokecherry
and purpled clusters
of wild grapes,
pulsating with ceremonial wine.

Her ruby blood drained
from tangy plum,
the scarlet crab apple
and crimson cherry,
until sacrificial vats
were filled to overflowing.

Now all across my kitchen sill,
winter's sun,
aflame on frosted window,
laces rainbow halos
through summer's sacrifice,
resurrected in crystal glasses.

The Leveling

Paragons of plenty, they swept regally
into the x-ray waiting room,
reeking of wealth, if not of health.

Their hair scrolled in coiled knots,
each strand a prism of perfection,
they slipped off leather coats
draped over designer blouses
and Saks' slacks, and announced their
presence to the receptionist.

They settled primly on the drab
foam-cushioned couch, like two
china dolls, labeled "Don't Touch".
The technician, indifferent, beckoned
the older behind closed doors
to perform a magical transformation.

A tapestry unraveled, she rejoined
the prosaic assemble of patients,
wrinkled hospital gown
drooping deviously beneath the warped
hem of the ridiculous robe.

An aristocrat humbled,
leveled to reluctant communion
by mutual indignities.

Regret

Young mother asleep,
Cradled in satin,
Her gentle arms caress
And bind the infant to her bosom
For the long journey.

Before her coffin,
Flower garden of red roses
And Lily of the Valley,
I stand at last.
Guilt needles my heart.
It bleeds.

Though our contact so brief,
And more than ten years past,
I remember with gratitude
That day, for I lay helpless
On my bed with shattered ankle.
Friends came, some to help,
Others said, "If you need help
Let me know."
If you need help?
Eight children, two babies,
If you need help?

But she came, asking no price,
Used friend of the young man
Who worked for us.
Only thirteen, with willing hands,
Deer-like, bounding swiftly through dishes,
Floors, baking and crying babies.
Gentle, a child like my children,
Motherless, yet I mothered not.

Oh, yes, I was grateful,
That is in my favor,
"Thank you, thank you," I told her,
But I didn't mention You, Lord,
After all, she had been to church,
She had a father, didn't she?
Was I to blame he didn't care?
Oh, Lord, forgive me!

Fifteen, she married,
You know, that kind of marriage,
But not to our young man
Who stole her virtue
With false ardor.
Babies, divorce,
Remarriage, to an ex-con,
More babies, at last
One too many,
To nestle like a doll asleep
In little girl arms.

Only you, Lord, can comprehend
Why death was allowed
To sabotage the countdown.

I wish I could tell her now
How much I loved her
For her kindness to me
When I was down.
Oh, God, how I wish I could tell her
What I thought so many times,
But I come too late,
She lies deaf in her coffin.

A timorous cough
Pervades my thoughts.
Oh, yes, I'm standing here
Too long.
Her relatives and friends
Stare at me,
Who is this stranger
Who stands so long?

I must move on.
Why stand here now,
When all these years
I had no time
To come?

Three score and ten
The years of man,
Not a score and five.
Oh, God, if only I had known
She would die
So soon.

What My Grandmothers Taught Me

What did my grandmothers teach me,
those paragons of unconditional love?
of course, as most grandmothers do,
they taught me many necessary things,
like how to clean a wooden floor
without streaks, how and when to sweep,
and how to clean blue crockery bowls,
whose sides grew sticky from mixing dough
for bread, how to set a table,
and how to hem a skirt, though I never
learned to sew I must confess.

They taught me hospitality; their tables
had always room for dearest friends
or strangers who stopped by,
for feasts or just a piece of cake
and china cups of tea.
From them I learned the need of kitchens;
cookies shaped as chickens, cows or bears,
buttered yeast foam bread, sliced thick,
and spread with sugar or tasty rhubarb jam,
served with shares of Grandma's love
and fascinating tales of years gone by,
that taught me why and who I am.

They taught me charity as I watched them,
from their own meager stores,
share a cup of peas, a slice of bread,
with hungry widows come to beg for more.
And in the end, I learned to not fear death.
My grandmothers died just as they had lived,
and trusting their Lord with faithful hearts
they went smiling from this world to the next.

A grandmother asked of me a shocking thing,
"My grandchildren, how do I make them love me?"

I could not answer, I only know the mind
can never learn what is a matter of the heart,
and I am grateful, that by their examples,
my grandmothers in my youthful years,
so molded me that I myself today can be
a truly loved and loving grandmother.

A Day With Rebecca

The playground equipment
was all still there,
although the cottonwood
and oak were bare,
when Rebecca, who was five,
and I, who was threescore
and ten years older,
went to the park in late October.
We played all morning
until way past noon
for we knew that winter
would be coming soon,
and the wind would
blow much colder.

And no one else was there,
to stare or care.

We swung on the swings
like birds with wings,
the wind blew leaves in our eyes,
and we swung up,
and we swung high
and tried to touch
the geese flying by;
we rode the rocking horses;
though I sat my weight light,
we pretended we were cowboys
on a dark and rainy night
yodeling and making lots of noise
stopping a cattle stampede
on our swift steeds.

And no on else was there
to stare or care.

We swigged a drink of water
then headed for the teeter-totter,
Rebecca sat on one end,
I stood on the other
and bend by bend
like a good grandmother,
I balanced her weight
and landed her straight
until we spied the slippery slide.
We both climbed up
and looked around,
then we both slid down,
not side by side –
my bottom was much too wide.
We laughed like clowns
all the way down,
and landed in the dirt,
without getting hurt.

And no one else was there
to stare or care.

We ran to wind
the merry-go-round,
until the speed was right,
oh, we were a sight
as we leaped off the ground,
and rode the merry-go-round,
around and around
until it ran down.
Too soon a storm cloud hid the sun,
sleet pinged our faces like splinters,
the north wind whispered of winter,
warned us to run,
and that ended our fun.

And no one else was there
to stare or care.

Oh, we were wild all day,
we went to a ritzy cafe,
all messy and cold from play.
The waiter rolled his eyes,
while we ordered shrimp and fries
and hot chocolate, jumbo size.
My poor old body hurt,
so we refused dessert,
and hurried home
while we were still alert
and collapsed on the playroom couch.
I rested by arthritic ouch,
and Rebecca took her nap
with her brown curls on my lap.

And no one else was there
to know or care.

Loaves Of Love

Our small town guardian angel,
was baker of blue ribbon bread,
and sure as morning brings sunrise
she assembled her brown crock bowl,
her bent tins of flour, overflowing
with creamy unbleached, and whole wheat
freckled with nutty-gold graham.

The sweet mushy liquid from last night's
potatoes she heated lukewarm
in her blue granite kettle, and
quenched the thirst of her special
ingredients in the brown crock bowl.
Flour puffs frosted the front of her dress,
and drifted in clouds to the floor,

as her strong-knuckled fingers kneaded
the dough, until its texture turned smooth
as baby cheeks, and gas bubbles
snapped like fire crackers on the 4th of July.
Lovingly swaddled in pansy print towels,
the mound of dough climbed the slope of bowl
until she kneaded it down, let it rise again,

then patted fat loaves into tarnished
tin pans, and covered it all with the
pansy print towels for rising. She
lighted a match to yesterday's news,
igniting dry twigs and cottonwood chips,
glittered with bits of coal,
until the blue Monarch range fanned fire

in its throat and the cooktop smoked from
bacon-spattered mornings. The thermostat
needle on the closed oven door crept slowly
to proper degree; and baking well done

in the Monarch's belly, the russet brown loaves
launched "come hither" aromas out open windows
on summer's midmorning town-crier breeze.

On cue, the neighborhood children
invaded her kitchen, and chattering
like affectionate squirrels,
claimed their places at the table,
as our small town guardian angel
served up slices of love, spread
thick with butter and wild plum jam.

A Dress For Granddaughter's Wedding

I sweat my way through racks without end,
smothered by inelegant fashions,
rayon, pure silk, and all kinds of blends,
stitched together in confusing creations.

Though I came quite willing to spend,
sale prices still leave me upset,
but I have other problems to solve,
like deciding what color to get,
dark shades, champagne or mauve?

Waistlines are snugged with elastic,
or buttons, while some even zip,
young fashions promote a mid-thigh squeeze
that accentuates lean hips,
a bit risque for even this Granny,
do cover my cellulite, please!

Column dresses hug derrieres,
with rear slits high as my fanny,
invitation to unwanted stares!

String straps and cleavage bosoms,
cut so low it is hard to believe,
I am not tempted to buy them,
I don't have that much to cleave.

My legs too weary for one step more,
I search the mall in growing distress,
until I sneak into the Goodwill store
in a flash of bold inspiration,
and find me a dress, a suitable dress,
a made for a wedding creation.

Shuttling Grandma

Sad day in Norfolk, the day when
Grandma, sliding uphill past eighty,
like a reluctant child giving away
a favorite toy, decided to relinquish
her keys; death sentence to her greatest joy,
tooling around town in her 1988
Cadillac DeVille, exchanging freedom
for humility of mobile frustration.

Fantasies of youthful exuberance, no
more, ditto for driving around town,
windows rolled down, long scarf
snapping in the wind; like a sailor
banned from the sea, sentenced to
lubbing on land, she struggles with
the boundaries of irksome routines.

She, who maneuvered the Interstate
and urban traffic with ease, who once
could dash out to lunch with a friend,
or to the mall on spontaneous whim,
now demoted to arranging for rides;
suffers a twinge of green-eyed regret,
when she sees other drivers tool around
town, in her 1988 Cadillac DeVille.

Unlike local appointments, arranged
with comparative ease, when arthritis
attacks, and pain relief is sparse, then
the Arthritis Clinic in Lincoln come
hither, and complications are
numerous indeed; children, gung-ho to
honor her needs, must solve the
question that arises, who will be chosen
to shuttle Grandma to Lincoln, and
deliver her back home?

Renewal

Wrap your arms around me, Spring,
Warm these aching bones
Crying out in weariness of winter.
Erase the pain of snow-blind eyes
With soft green leaves
And yellow daffodils.
Then wake my fallow heart
With April rains,
That love might grow again.

Nightmares

Wrapped in soft folds
of night's darkness,
weary minds reject sleep,
pondering decisions
that well could keep
until morning light.

Even we who know
the promise best,
"Come unto me
all you who are weary",
surely we could rest!

Cabin Fever

Cabin fever usually attacks where snow
piles high outside the door; wind the only
company, wailing melancholy tunes under
the eaves on lonesome nights; when snow rides
the pine boughs down to crack the frigid quiet.

Only an inquisitive deer or two, famished
mountain lions searching for a meal, eagles
keening aloft in ice blue skies, or hungry hawks
wheeling down to snatch an unsuspecting mouse,
break the winter solitude,

Seclusion often nurtures spiritual musings.
But when all the books have been read,
elk and black bean soup the only diet,
and the outside world of humans is a memory,
then desolate moods usually intrude.

Cabin fever does not need isolation to
sneak in; fed by long nights crowding out days,
blustery winters of bleakness, and snow plows
shooting gray-streaked white piles along
slushy streets, the sickness tarries.

Traffic din roars by, cell phones ring, the postman
comes, and crowds brush shoulders in passing,
people everywhere, yet this malady persists,
this lumbago of the spirit; victims pray for
the only cure, the fresh warm breath of early spring.

The house-bound arthritic walker brigade,
losing battles with slippery walks and snowdrifts
too steep to climb, wave to escapees trudging by,
read large print books over chicken noodle soup,
wrestle winter doldrums with dreams of summertime.

The Accommodating Accomplice

Forty years, my farmer and I
lived in a country house,
high on a grassy hill,
thrived on mutual devotion,
listened to moo of cows,
and crack of growing corn,
dawn's crowing rooster
our thrifty alarm.

The day we exchanged
the peace of country lanes
for bustle of city streets,
our life pattern scrambled.
Between sunset and sunrise,
tired farmer was mine,
sunrise to sunset I waited,
alone and hermit-lonely.

Longing for life more exciting
than Queen of solitaire,
I discovered an accomplice,
so compatible, understanding,
such as I had never known,
one to whom I entrusted
my burden, a grievance that
had stressed me for years.

The relationship seemed
surely blessed. Then,
to my dismay, that on which
I doted left, and did not
even say goodbye.
I hastened to find another,
equally accommodating
to relieve my distress.

At last, my farmer,
tormented by suspicion,
discovered my indiscretions,
and did his best to bear
his irretrievable loss.

I confessed, my true intention
was not some deceitful plan,
I was simply delighted
with my garbage man,
and his garbage-eating truck,
that growls through the alley
on Wednesday morning, ravenous
for my eclectic buffet of trash.

J. Willy Wunder And Model T

J. Willy Wunder was quite a man,
he lived his life according to plan,
for whether the day was cool or hot,
he would work when others would not.
In fact, he worked his life away,
until his whiskers turned to grey.

He owned an ancient Model T,
every bit as tough as he,
and on his farm just south of town,
his garden rows ran up and down.
When other folks were still in bed,
he was picking cabbage heads,
crisp radishes and turnip greens,
red tomatoes, green-yellow beans,
white onions, carrots, baby beets,
and ears of corn, the sweetest sweet;
all this by noon he would deliver.

His ancient Model T, sixty-three,
was one score younger than was he;
while other folks would stop to play,
he and his flivver worked all day;
fencing to keep his milk cows in,
hauling feed to his laying hens,
they plowed, and hoed and fertilized,
all day long they exercised.
His trusty flivver's time was spent,
everywhere J. Wunder went,
his main repairs were old tin cans,
but his ancient flivver always ran.

J. Wunder reached one hundred two,
still finding lots of things to do,
and still, by noontime, would deliver
produce in his trusty flivver.

One winter night at ten past seven,
J. Wunder died and went to heaven;
the people searched all up and down,
the little farm just south of town,
but not a trace or piece could see
of J. Willy Wunder's Model T.

Just watch the ziggy flashing lights,
that streak the sky on stormy nights,
for when the heavens rumble loud,
they're busy banging through the clouds,
still working hard, J. Willy Wunder
and his trusty flivver making thunder.

Oracle On Oracles

My pet peeve
is folks
who give advice on everything
from egg yolks
to child psychology,
and would advise
the best procedure
which applies
to raising kids.

They leave me charred,
since most "oracles" couldn't pin
a rear guard
on baby's crucial area,
but profess to know
what makes his complicated
system go.

They cloud the cradle
with dire predictions,
and spew advice
with contradictions,
while high rises the tide
of tongue waves
wagging mothers
to early graves.

I love advice
from parents
of one or many,
since they're most often
wise enough
not to give any.

Unrequited Love

Sentient the souls that own
an inborn love of sea,
whose heartbeats pulse
in rhythm with crash of waves
on rocky shores, and even though
their feet are planted in prairie soil,
a restless longing haunts their days,
and they know a certain telepathy
with the shining sea.

Strawberry Pie

When I am an old lady,
a soon tomorrow,
I will sit at the lunch counter
in pink sweat pants
and cranberry jacket.
I will eat strawberry pie,
and sit by my old lady friend
who delights in banana cream.
And when some busy-body asks,
as I did today,
"Is it good?"
I will take my time,
and answer later,
much later,
if at all,
"Yes, it is."
And go on eating
my strawberry pie.

The Catalyst

I used to think that writer's block,
was an imaginary bunch of crock,
and anyone at anytime could make a rhyme
and pick a subject from a thousand inspirations
that came to mind. But I find a muscle relaxant
has hit my brain, and I try creating all in vain.

I look out my window at the maple tree branches,
leaves lying dead-still, as if in a trance, until
north wind persuades them to join him in dance.
The cardinal feasting at the feeder so long,
is inspired to burst into joyous song,
while my brain lies dormant as a bear in his den,
impervious to what it has formerly been.

What spark can return it to that fertile time,
when it was brimming with rhythm and rhyme?
Yes!! How clear to me now, the viable solution,
to revive this dried-up river of thought
the perfect catalyst to break this writer's block!
Let me drink of the cup of invigoration,
to access the fountain of my inspirations,
to sweep me at last, past mental sedation,
on to enthusiasm and the joy of creation.

I prefer Folgers without hesitation.

Elegy for Memorial Day

We come today to honor the dead
of our nations' wars.
To humbly grieve that evil lusts
of greedy minds threaten the homes
and lives of liberty loving peoples,
who then must fight to save
the freedom they so cherish.

We remember not only the dead, who rest
in peace, but also those in silent halls
forgotten, who lie an endless day on beds
of pain, and wait to die. They, too,
have given their lives for our land,
and for freedom stood their ground, to lift
common people to the level of kings.

They proudly fought and died, to preserve
our precious heritage of the right to vote,
the right to be a small heard voice
to govern this great land of ours.
A grateful people who thanked their God
that they were free from tyrant's rule,
and no dictator made a mockery of their will.

God forbid that we accept, without challenge,
a loss of our rights, or accept a handout
instead of tightening our belts, to deter
our people from exchanging our freedom
for the power and rule of state,
and the possible tyranny of evil men,
to bequeath our children only chains.

It is expedient that we muzzle complacency,
no matter what the sacrifice,
and keep, unshackled by corruption,
our gift of freedom, in gratitude to those

who gave their lives to hold it high,
lest their blood cry up from every
bloodstained battlefield, and condemn us,
that we have let them die in vain.

Meditations Of An Old Mother

My body lies wrinkled
and dying.
Weariness beats hard on me.
My bones rebel at a near century
of servitude,
and disease pummels me for my tenacity.

And you, the babies that I nurtured
at my breast,
snow on your crowns,
the ravages of age bending you also
like gnarled trees
in life's relentless winds,
why do you weep?

Do you weep
because of sorrowed affection
for an old mother dying,
or because truth visits you
in this vigil that you keep
around my deathbed,
and as you hover close to me
you feel the years pulling your cold feet
under my covers?

Fear not.
Though you must be as I am now,
at peace await the Sower's coming
to reap His hard harvest,
and with joy exchange this pitiful existence
for a lovelier certainty.

Pain

Might I know again
the sweet deep sleep of youth;
night renewing tired bodies,
basking in the rising sun,
at morning's awakening
eager to begin the day's journey.

Alone in the tedious night,
pain steals my sleep,
controls my old body,
immune to potency of pills,
offering no pardon,
no turning back time.

Pain is the Lord's way,
to prepare my spirit
to vacate this worn-out
residence with joy.
In the meantime, in His mercy,
he sends a temporary reprieve
from my present affliction,
purging it in my heating pad's fire.

Devotion

Patriarch of progeny who wing the seas
and journey home from near and distant lands,
how foolish to define your neutered ego
so unwisely. Why measure our devotion

by passion's fire, when true affection from
our alpha to omega years sustains our
precious waning hours, and satisfies with
pleasures far more lasting than desire?

Newly-wedded ecstasy has never rung
wild bells forever; let mellowed hearts compose
euphonies of love that nurture with finesse
their golden jubilees.

Such love as savors sharing of communion
cup, that gently clasps arthritic fingers
touching in the night, and searches laughter
crinkled eyes to claim a kiss.

Love that treasures tear-jerk memories that
linger still of newly-married ardor,
subdued by wonderment at babies wailing,
fresh from the womb.

Love that walked with weariness from tender
cares that knew no scheduled hour, and spawned
a lifelong vigil that consumed the years and
brought us here to sunset all too soon.

Release without regret, my love, our passionate
afternoon, and together let us venture, hand
in hand, into the sunset's swiftly fading light,
for yonder, not too far, beckons the Morning Star.

Let It Be Spring

Oh, Lord, let it be spring,
or early autumn;
let gentle breezes blow
when they lay me in my grave.
Let no blinding snow
in frigid north winds rave.

Let those who come not need
a grave side tent to shield
from winter's bitter storm,
or need to huddle close
to keep the children warm.

Although I wouldn't mind a tear or two,
let happy communications sound
as they begin to leave,
to wander down to funeral feast.
Only let them remember that I believed.

Later on, if they have time,
let them plant a yellow rose or two.
If not, dandelions and wild violets
or even a mantle of grass will do.
The grave is a temporary thing, I know;
still, Lord, let it be spring when I go.

Farewell To A Dear Friend

I looked at you, my friend,
in the nursing home,
and did not see a woman
old and failing, body shrinking,
reclining on four-wheeled gurney,
like some small child,
too young for long walks.

I did not hear a mind
that flowed in and out,
like endless tides
on a sea of memories,
nor did I dwell on restless fingers
fumbling, winding the coverlet
into bunches, over and over.

When I looked at you, my friend,
I saw your graceful body dancing,
I heard your happy voice
and ever joyous laughter.
I saw you teaching children,
delighting in their happy times,
offering solace for their tears,
transfusing hearts with gifts of love,
remembered long years after.

Even then, I knew
this time would come,
when I must say farewell,
and weep my tears of sorrow.
Yet, I would not hold you here;
for gentle the angels
who escorted you home
to paradise, and there, took away
your heartache, your pain,
and wiped the tears from your eyes.

Oh, what exaltation you must know,
singing praises to your Lord,
dancing in those golden streets,
and, oh, my friend, once again,
like celestial carillons, sounding
your ever-joyous laughter.

About the Author

Dorthy Knouse Koepke, poet, author, and speaker, was born January 24, 1922, in Kingsbury County, South Dakota, the oldest girl in a family of nine children. She was raised in South Dakota and began writing when she was 12 years old. Her first poem was published when she was only 16.

She finished eighth grade in 1935 and spent the next three years at home caring for her younger siblings. At age 16, she began High School in Cavour, South Dakota, while working for a couple for room and board. Through this couple she met her future husband.

In 1942, she graduated High School as valedictorian. She attended Huron College for one year and majored in journalism. Dorthy was assistant editor of the college paper and secretary-treasurer of her sorority, Pi Alpha Phi. Although she received two scholarships to attend college, she had to work a variety of jobs to make ends meet. Two such jobs included washing dishes at the bus stop for twenty-five cents an hour, and writing several features for the Evening *Huronite* newspaper.

In 1990, she was named Alumnus of the Month by Huron University in Huron, South Dakota.

Dorthy married Herman in 1943, and moved to Hoskins, Nebraska. Raising ten kids kept her too busy to become worldly famous but gave her more than enough inspiration and ideas for writing fodder, from which she created hundreds of poems and stories.

In addition to writing, she listed her occupations as Manager & Bookkeeper for the Koepke Farm, and Enthusiastic Mother of Ten Children.

She has written, published, and received numerous honors and awards in local and national venues for many of her poems and short stories. A poem "Dust Bowl," won first place in a national contest and received praise from Bill Kloefkorn, State Poet of Nebraska, who once called it "an example of a perfect poem." She has also written a children's book, which is yet unpublished.

She satisfied her desire to return to school by attending writer's workshops, seminars and conferences. After attending the Billy Graham School of Christian Writing in 1969, she wrote an article for the Norfolk, Nebraska newspaper about her days at the Billy Graham School. She described her return home from this wonderful experience by saying, "Back home again, daily struggling through the vortex of tornadic activity created by my husband and seven still-at-home children, I am even more determined to be one of the crew on my Savior's Rocketship."

Many times, day and night, healthy or sick, washing clothes or dishes, cooking mountains of food, tending children, husband, and relatives, or milking cows, she would be reciting poetry, or stopping all of a sudden to quick jot down a note or idea, or write a new poem just composed in her mind. She squeezed in writing time at her desk and typewriter in the "study," which often was just a bedroom with several beds, a crib, and a dresser.

Her poetry is an intimate look at her thoughts and feelings as a farm wife, mother and faithful disciple of God. After reading her poetry, grandson, Jesse Koepke, writes: "I feel like I know her so much better. It was an intimate trip through her thoughts and her life. She's very honest in her writing, and writes it in such a way that's accessible."

She gives some of the credit for her writing abilities to her grandmother who hailed from York, England, and was a storyteller with a keen sense of humor.

She is a member of the Spindrift Poets Club in Norfolk, Nebraska, as well as the Nebraska Chaparral Poets, of which she has served on the executive board. She has been a member of the National Writers Club and the Society of Children's book writers.

Her work has been published in *Midwest Living Magazine, Highlights for Children, Christian Science Monitor, Guidepost Magazine, Magazine of the Midlands, Grit Magazine, Whole Notes, Midwest Poetry Review, National Writer's Club, This Day Magazine, Nebraska Center for the Book, Lutheran Witness, Celebrate - University of Nebraska-Omaha, and South Dakota State Poetry Society - Pasque Petals.*

In 1996, she traveled to Anaheim, California, at the invitation of the Famous Poets Society, to read her poem, "Resurrection" at the Famous Poets Convention.

In 2002, she received first place in the Nebraska Mother's Association and the Mother's Association, Inc., in the essay division of the literature contest with her story "The Real Christmas."

Dorthy's book, *Love Made Me Do It*, published in 1984, has been distributed in over 30 states.